"You will recognize yourself, your family, and your friends in these true stories, and find that prayer can be an opportunity to see things in a different way."

—Lyn Klug, editor/compiler, *All Will Be Well: A Gathering of Healing Prayers*, *SoulWeavings: A Gathering of Women's Prayers*, and *A Forgiving Heart: Prayers for Blessing and Reconciliation*

"In the sixties, when we all ran hard, Boyd taught us to run with Jesus. Now, he teaches us to walk, don't run, to the exit. He gives one hand to Jesus, then takes our hand as we stumble home."

—The Rt. Rev. Paul Moore, Jr., Bishop of New York (retired)

"Once again, in *Prayers for the Later Years*, Malcolm Boyd has shown so beautifully how he doesn't just write prayers. First, he writes wonderful vignettes about people. And, in doing so, he makes us better both understand people and appreciate God."

—Frank Deford, author and commentator

"Thirty years ago, when I could still run, I found Boyd's *Are You Running with Me, Jesus?* a wonderful companion. This new book will be a wise and challenging friend now that I've slowed down to a dignified walk. I especially appreciate Boyd's honest, balanced perspective on leaning into elderhood."

—Dr. Carl Koch, Program Coordinator at The Franciscan Spirituality Center, Director, MA in Servant Leadership Program at Viterbo University, author, *God Knows You'd Like a New Body: 12 Ways to Befriend the One You've Got* and other books

"Boyd's book offers the wisdom of a life prayed through many seasons. His example shows us how to pray our own lives, and inspires courage to make fresh choices."

—Marilyn McCord Adams, Horace Tracy Pitkin Professor of Historical Theology, Yale Divinity School

"The older we get the more we pray and the greater our need for helpers in prayer. In this book, one member of 'the greatest generation' continues to be the prayer partner he has been for many of us since we asked in our youth, 'Are you running with me, Jesus?'"

—The Rev. Paul Wennes Egertson, Ph.D., Senior Lecturer in Religion, California Lutheran University, Thousand Oaks, Calif.; Bishop Emeritus, Southwest California Synod, ELCA

Also by Malcolm Boyd

PRAYERS
for the LATER
YEARS

MALCOLM BOYD

Augsburg
MINNEAPOLIS

CONTENTS

I want to thank:

A select group of women and men in their own later years who became role models of aging for me and generously taught me the rudiments of growing older by their examples.

Many readers of my published work—living in different parts of the United States and often abroad—who have kindly responded in a most active way by writing remarkably honest letters that have never failed to inform and challenge me, as well as offer fresh insights and new ways of looking at life's variety of choices and dilemmas.

Martha Rosenquist, my indefatigable editor, who not only asked me to write this book, but sagaciously suggested its title. Our work relationship has been a refreshing delight and a spiritual bonding.

Mark Thompson, for abiding wisdom and support.

⌇

"When the conflicting currents of the unconscious create engulfing whirlpools, the waters can again be guided into a single current if the dam sluice be opened into the channel of prayer—and if that channel has been dug deep enough."

—Dag Hammarskjöld, *Markings*

INTRODUCTION

As I write these lines, my own life is slowing down considerably. Its pace has changed from high energy running to a more reflective and measured walking in my gradual approach to my eightieth birthday. Yet the dynamic of prayer in my life grows ever stronger.

Many people might look casually at a life like mine and perceive it as settled, basically over, secure and serene, and certainly without pressing decisions to make. This view is incorrect and immature.

Older life is alive with possibilities, marked by many changes, and confronted by a brace of problems. The latter range from physical to psychological, and include financial, motivational, spiritual, relational, the enduring question of meaning itself, and how to prepare for dying and death.

Recently I felt that I must make a hard decision about where to put my limited time and energy. However, just when it seemed absolutely clear to me exactly what I should do, I found myself looking at a brick wall. Nothing "gave." I felt lost, a victim of circumstances, shaken by anxiety. I wished for a rudder, something tangible to hold onto. What should I do? I prayed quietly and resolutely.

Then, quite suddenly, a door opened onto a completely unsuspected and unknown alternative. I was led in a fresh direction I had never dreamed of. My prayer was being answered in an astonishingly beneficent way. There seemed to be a single requirement that I was asked to honor: Give up. Give up control. Let go. Let God.

God has been in my consciousness, and Jesus a close companion, since the start of my memory: a familiar and comforting and challenging presence, an anchor and solid rock, the ultimate source of being and security.

When I was five years old I wrote my first prayer. Because my mother saved it—mothers love to do things like that—I still have it:

Your Holy father is in your temple
a temple is when your good pray
and thank your Holy father
for what God is doing all the time
for your Holy father gives
you the world and a home clothes
water air food you should thank
God for it at least five times a
day everybody should love their
Holy father God. Amen.

As my relationship with God changed and deepened over the years, so did my prayer. During college days of rebellion I believed that I was turning away from God. At that time my prayer became more occasional, tending to occur in isolated moments of crisis or sharply felt need.

Later, as an adult approaching midlife, I seemed to talk and talk and talk and talk to Jesus in my prayers. I realize these weren't simply narcissistic monologues but reflections of an honest yearning and seeking for truth. Over subsequent years I've tended to grow quieter, to wait—and listen. The key, I have discovered, is to relinquish the illusion of control in moments when I'd prefer to blurt out to Jesus: "Why can't it be my way? Why don't you just give me what I want and am sure is best for me?"

I have lived through hard turning points in my life when God completely surprised me by leading me in directions I had no intention of moving. One was journeying to Hollywood after college, finding myself in the motion picture and early TV industry. This hadn't seemed to be in the cards at all. I felt totally unprepared for it.

Another was my departure from Hollywood in 1951 to enter a theological seminary and prepare for the Episcopal priesthood. I asked Jesus, in some alarm and trepidation: "Why are you doing this to me? How can I possibly do what you're asking?"

Life was tough indeed in my first parish in the inner-city of Indianapolis. There was no heat in the old church building during some harsh wintry days; women and men who attended services needed to wear coats, hats, and gloves while they were inside the freezing structure. The roof leaked. The congregation was tiny and often hurting. I asked: "Jesus, what do you have in mind here? Could you please let me know?"

I was aware in those days of racism as a deadly virus in the nation's body, but the problem had been remote from my experience until 1961 when I was asked to join a Freedom Ride in the deep south to protest apartheid practices in the United States. I was scared to go, feeling I lacked the courage. I sat in a chair all night in a darkened room and prayed. I asked for guidance, sweating and waiting. The next morning it seemed clear I must go. This changed my life forever, moving me toward goals of justice, and providing me stamina and discipline, hope and faith, to persevere.

In 1965 I wrote my first book of prayers, titled *Are You Running with Me, Jesus?* Since that time I have written more, most recently in *Running with Jesus.* I find prayer something of a miracle and also absolutely ordinary. Sometimes when I am literally wrestling with God in prayer (a bit like Jacob wrestling with the angel) it helps me to practice deep breathing. So, when I am hiking in the hills, which I frequently do, I may breathe consciously with a bird flying overhead in the sky. Or breathe with a tree under whose branches I sit, or with a flowing stream of water.

At other times in the city I breathe with other people in a crowd—the humanity for whom Jesus Christ died and rose from the dead. At certain moments I am aware God breathes in me, even as I breathe with God.

Suddenly, all of life becomes a prayer as I begin to see Christ figures wherever people are: on the street, at work, at home; lonely, hungry, addicted, wounded; happy, laughing, dancing, in repose.

I believe that prayer is essentially being present with God in a conscious way: silently, speaking, listening, asking, giving thanks, worshipping.

The prayers that follow are written in, and for, the later years.

GROWING
OLDER ৯৭

WHEN I WAS FORTY, FIFTY, EVEN SIXTY, I hadn't the least idea what it meant to grow old.

Meanwhile, however, I kept on growing older. There were changes in my body, mind, and spirit. Certain limitations and boundaries made their appearance. I couldn't understand them very well at first.

But then, with an onslaught of ever new aches and pains, problems and needed subsequent decisions, I got the message. I was growing older. These prayers are about that.

I have learned, in my own life, that growing older is perhaps the greatest blessing I have experienced. It is a time to forgive, to mellow, to understand, to make peace, and to figure out what life is all about. So it is a time of reflection and wonder, humor and grace—if we let it be. This becomes the finest legacy we can pass on to others.

Where did summer go, Jesus? What happened to last year? Time is racing.

An engagement for next Tuesday sneaked up on me. I had completely forgotten it until I noticed it scrawled on my calendar. It's all something of a hodgepodge. . . .

Can I stop the rush of events and things to do, Jesus? Apparently not. But I can try to stay calm within the storm, prioritize duties on the basis of their significance, fence off quiet times, and keep my own pace manageable.

I can't run anymore, Jesus. Thank you for understanding this. I appreciate your matching your pace to mine when we walk together.

Thanks for walking with me, Jesus. Thanks for just staying here quietly with me.

Thanks for rescuing me, Jesus. I was on a total downbeat. Aches and pains caught up with me. My arthritis hurt badly. There was a new flare-up in my knee. Then I felt an onslaught of self-pity, and on top of everything else I couldn't get a good night's sleep.

I looked like hell because I felt like hell. I was fatigued, without a spring to my step or an ability to laugh at anything. I felt I'd become a bore to other people, talking endlessly about my pains and problems.

Just then you stirred me out of my lethargy when you guided a good friend to remind me that I may be old in years but needn't be in attitude.

Soon I stopped whining and said "Yes" to an offer of volunteer work. The fresh project energized me, made me feel valuable and needed, brought me into a community with other people, and I was on my way.

Your own example of selflessness, hard work, and love of people continues to inspire me with hope, Jesus.

Different people's reactions to my age can be upsetting, Jesus.

One reaction is to sentimentalize me as an older person. I am seen as folkloric, inherently funny, essentially childish, harmless, and quite unnecessary.

Another response is one of anger and frustration. If, for example, I am moving slowly and in the way of someone who wants to move faster, I am criticized. The message is: If you can't keep up, then at least have the decency to drop out.

Yet another reaction is to offer help to an image of myself as infirm, muddled, poised on the brink of collapse, and a threat to the common good.

However, I am simply me, Jesus. Thanks to your example and teachings, I take myself seriously in the scheme of things. I am grateful that my life matters and I am significant in your love.

It helps to know that I have gifts to offer. One is my awareness that life in the fast lane can be a killer, while a more reflective pace permits greater sensitivity, understanding, and loving.

I wish more people could understand this, Jesus.

Some of my happiest moments are found when I am out in nature, Jesus. I love the sky, sun, formations of clouds, hills, winding dirt paths, heights, stones, shrubs, and wild flowers.

Yet I am fondest of trees. I sit beneath them in wonder, delight, and security. Although a number of people might find me eccentric or a bit crazy, I talk to trees. They seem to possess the wisdom of the ages. Talk about maturity! They have it all. They have weathered the seasons gracefully, spread their branches beneficently, given their leaves without stint, and been present in the midst of life with utter vulnerability.

My mind clears when I walk or hike in nature. My body forgets aches and pains. My spirit dances and soars. A gentle rain or breeze on my face is a blessing. Other people whom I meet on a path or a hill are seekers like me.

I feel incredibly alive here, Jesus, in the midst of creation.

I left everything in a shambles, Jesus. I was tired. This left me with zero tolerance for human error, a seeming slight, or the least suggestion of a crisis.

Then, a crisis emerged (or seemed to) around a community project I'm a part of. Anger surfaced in the group along with sharp differences of opinion. Voices were raised, including mine. Old animosities, long swept under the rug, emerged in a loud and conflicting way.

I found myself in the middle of this bad situation. (I was as unpleasant and demanding as anyone else present.) I attempted to give the appearance of rising above the fray. After all, couldn't I make it clear I am not a difficult or obstreperous person? Yet my actions made a mockery of my pretensions and contradicted my words.

Now many fences need mending, Jesus. Unity has to be restored, apologies offered and received, the work of healing begun. Please help me to stay centered, balanced, kind, peaceful, and quiet.

I sit here offering advice to someone half my age. I recognize his fear and anxiety, ego and ambition, wounds and pains, joy and laughter, his trepidation about facing the future. This, from my own nearly identical life experiences in the past.

The room is very quiet. I listen carefully as he speaks. It seems an eternal story with contemporary modifications. He needs assurance, strength to go on, a chance to laugh and perhaps to cry in a moment of painful self-realization. I need to convey the presence of hope, renewed commitment to life, and the need for courage. I want him to comprehend that my counsel's substance is rooted in God's love.

So, I delve into my memory and history. Where—and when—have I been in terms of where he is now? What was the situation? The cast of characters? Looking back, did I seem to find a discernible right or wrong? I try to suggest changes he may be able to make in his life that will positively affect his future.

While we sit here together, struggling to understand what you want, please guide us, Jesus.

I had a difficult time this morning getting out of bed, Jesus. I didn't want to. I had rolled over into a very comfortable position, my head rested sublimely on a soft pillow. I wanted nothing at that moment to do with the day's demands.

Needless to say, I got out of bed. When I walked into the bathroom, I contemplated my routine including a shower, a shave, and the seemingly endless ritual of toothbrushing. (I've done it all my life! Can't I stop now?)

In the midst of such ruminations, I caught sight of my face in the mirror over the basin. Clearly, I wasn't prepared to like myself very much this morning.

However, I found myself surprised when I greeted me with equanimity. Realizing I liked me, I mustered a warm smile. The smile looked good. I liked me even better.

The day was going to be fine, after all. I accepted me, and it, and you, Jesus.

What is maturity, Jesus? Is it found in life's experiences, years lived, people known, and lessons learned? If so, it appears that I possess some maturity.

But do others recognize it?

Forgive my self-pity, but I want to receive some credit for my maturity. My self-esteem needs it. If other people fail to acknowledge my achievement, I can easily feel undervalued. My very worth comes into question.

Yet doesn't my maturity come from you, Jesus? It is your gift. Thank you for it. Help me to feel grateful to you instead of needing recognition from others.

Honestly, it doesn't matter too much if others don't see my maturity when I know that you do, Jesus. Thank you for bonding with me and giving me your strength.

Moods, especially my own, confound me, Jesus. One day can seem serene and near perfect, the next fraught with perplexing problems or near disasters. In one hour I may appear kind and empathic, in the next harsh and intransigent.

Why?

It helps a lot to know that, in the course of my various ups and downs, you remain firmly loving and the trusted anchor of my life, Jesus. You do not stop loving me. You do not withdraw support when it's obvious I've disappointed you or failed you. You do not give up on me, calling me a failure, and move on to someone more serene and balanced, more spiritual and deserving.

Thank you for your presence in my life, Jesus. It helps to know I'm not alone. It helps to know I'm not unloved. It helps to know you are my eternal companion, lover, and savior.

Before very long, Jesus, I won't be here anymore. Sometimes I have trouble accepting this or dealing with it in a rational way. However, I know that I must. Yet this doesn't soften the situation or make it easier.

In one moment I'll still be present. In the next, however, I'll be gone. I suppose my problem is that I've become comfortable with life. Certainly, I know my way around. I take for granted all kinds of things, Jesus: fresh bread, small acts of kindness, rain on the roof at night, the newspaper on the steps in the morning, and familiar voices.

I guess I take for granted, too, my place in the human scene with its ups and downs, crazy turns, shifting moods, seasons and ironies, and a seeming permanence beneath it all.

However, that will suddenly be whisked away—like a rug pulled from under my feet—when I've died, my body has been burned, ashes scattered, possessions of a lifetime disposed of.

Stay with me, Jesus. Let me have your firm hand, the quietness of your presence, the thundering echo of your love.

CHANGES ॐ

ONE DAY I STARTED LOOKING AROUND ME at other people who were growing older as I was.

A great help was the thousands of letters I received in response to a column titled "You and I" that I wrote from 1990–2000 in AARP's *Modern Maturity* magazine. Men and women from every part of the United States, and the four corners of Earth, sent me mail. Usually they wrote on plain paper in longhand, expressions of honest feelings filling page after page.

I could visualize some of them seated at a kitchen table or an old wooden deck, addressing "Dear Malcolm" and following with their frank and realistic reactions to life.

Often they told me about changes taking place in their lives. These prayers concern changes like that.

Bertha is fed up, Jesus. Tired of feeling devalued as an older woman, denied dignity, being rudely treated as a stereotype: a "hysterical old lady" or an object of ridicule. She doesn't like being called "honey" by a clerk in a store or "Bertha" by a young receptionist in her dentist's office.

Enough! she says.

As I see it, Bertha needs to do more. She's got to communicate her feelings to all the other people directly involved in her life. They need to change the ways they have seen and treated her, along with their attitudes.

Because Bertha is not a stereotype, isn't it time for others to quit treating her like one, Jesus?

Ron, who is seventy-seven, explains that he fears aging, growing older, and growing old.

He works out at a fitness center three times a week, thirty minutes on a bike, thirty minutes on a treadmill, and fifteen minutes lifting weights. However, he doesn't like the way his knees are tightening up or his skin gets spottier.

Sometimes as he drives his car to a meeting he gets to thinking "How long will I be able to do this? What will happen then?" Ron says he doesn't know how to prepare for that. He feels that he lacks the necessary energy and motivation.

Work with Ron's thoughts and fears, Jesus. Help him to get ready for more changes.

Rosemary taught school for thirty-two years, welcoming the busyness, learning, human contacts, and the joy of helping children. She also luxuriated in the security of her husband and home.

But now, with all that gone, she feels stripped to the bone, Jesus. Her husband died a short while ago after both of them retired.

At seventy-two, she has children and grandchildren whom she loves. But she feels that she has lost life's meaning. She wonders: What can I do except draw the shades permanently?

It's hard, Jesus, when sudden change hits our lives without warning, scattering what we believed were our hopes, and leaving in shambles what we assumed was our security.

Yet our life continues. The sun comes up, trees stand, dogs bark, the evening news appears on TV. There are plants to water, bills to pay, people and challenges to meet, and prayers to pray. Please guide her to find meaning, Jesus.

One day Lionel realized he could easily turn into one of those unhappy people everybody hates to see coming up the street, Jesus. He was, in fact, on his way to being reclusive, enraged, sorry for himself, and inhospitable. A retired widower of seventy, he found few reasons to be happy.

I never found out exactly what made him decide his present style of life was a dead end. However, Lionel changed. Instead of being absent, he was present. Instead of being argumentative, he was friendly. It was quite a surprise to everybody who knew him.

Lionel's life turned around, Jesus. He thanks you.

Although she's been a widow for more than a year, Becky can't seem to emerge from a grieving pattern. Her friends are concerned. When they try to cheer her up or interest her in a new project, they seem to fail.

The more Becky thinks about her loss, she doesn't wish to see anyone. She says that she loved her husband with all her being and misses him terribly. It seems that after Becky created her own happy world, she assumed her happily married life would go on forever.

She cries much of the time. Can she come to understand that change is inevitable in human life? None of us can stand in its way or order it not to happen. Can Becky embrace change, Jesus?

What if you want to change your life, but think you can't? This is Vicky's question. She's sixty. Her finances are a shambles. Vicky is worn out from working.

If a man were to ask her for a date, she says she'd have to decline because she looks terrible, has nothing to wear, and would probably fall asleep by nine-thirty. As Vicky sees herself, she is depressed, always tired, and lonely as hell. Unless a miracle happens—like winning the state lottery—it appears she's sunk.

But I wonder, Jesus, why Vicky doesn't take the time to visit a thrift shop and pick out something nice to wear. Work on her appearance a bit. Invite someone to supper—and cook it. Wouldn't it be great if she could look at something funny and laugh, Jesus? Stay human, let hope have a chance, and not give up on life?

Tina grew tired of looking in a mirror. Shortly after she turned sixty-three, she tore up a set of her recent photographs because they showed her wrinkles and falling skin.

However, in the ensuing months, Tina has lost ten pounds, had a face-lift, and cut and dyed her hair because she'd always felt her mother was old at forty, and she decided not to go that route.

We're free, each one of us, to approach aging in our own way, aren't we, Jesus? It seems to me there is not only our outer appearance to be considered. Equally important is our interior life, how we define ourselves, what we ultimately desire.

In the past five years Michael has changed a lot. He's no longer an energetic professional but a disabled retiree at age fifty-nine. Surprisingly, he has never been happier, Jesus.

Being forced from a fast-paced treadmill to a snail-paced lifestyle has opened a new world for him. He's learned to really listen and appreciate other people for who they are instead of trying to fit them into professional molds.

Michael has come to accept himself as he is, with his limitations, and truly like himself as a human being. He no longer feels guilty if what he does isn't perfect, Jesus.

For more years than she cares to count, Liz was a person who listened, and listened, and listened. She was the one who always solved other people's problems. She picked up the pieces when other people's lives fell apart.

Liz was generally reliable, sturdy, dependable, and unselfish. Yet increasingly she felt like a doormat when friends appeared to take her generosity for granted.

A major turning point in Liz's life occurred recently when she contributed the heavy work on a community fund-raising drive. To her astonishment, someone else took public bows and applause for the job. Liz suddenly became aware this other person had talked, and talked, and talked—even as Liz had listened, and listened, and listened, and done the work.

Wouldn't it be a good idea, Jesus, if Liz started speaking up for herself?

Maureen awakened gradually to the awareness that her children were out of the house for good while her workaholic husband was totally involved in his job. Where did this leave her, Jesus?

She admitted that she had put her own needs and desires behind those of her kids and mate for twenty-some years. While this hurt, the situation grew far more serious when Maureen faced the reality that she'd also lost touch with herself.

Frankly, Maureen no longer knows what her own needs and desires are. Getting reconnected to herself is a huge, confusing task, Jesus.

For openers, could Maureen learn she doesn't have to knuckle under to every demand made on her?

OPENNESS
TO LIFE ॐ

I T SEEMS TO ME THAT ALL OF US HAVE A CHOICE: we can either lock ourselves inside a self-constructed cell that isolates us and separates us from the reality of living, or else we can decide to become vulnerable, celebrate our God-given humanness, and open up ourselves to God, other people, and life itself.

While this choice may seem hard at times, isn't it infinitely harder to shut ourselves away from God and life, joy and possibilities of grace?

These prayers are from people struggling creatively with this choice.

The worst way to confront death is to fear death; the worst way to confront life is to fear life. Openness to each is a first positive step.

They are lovers in their seventies, Jesus. They enjoy sex, feel loving, share friends, and might even elope one of these days.

But their children worry about them, think they're behaving like kids, and wish they would act in a more outwardly comforting way—that is, act their age. The children and their spouses don't begrudge their parents' having companionship, even a bit of fun. Yet when push comes to shove, they ask: Can't they just play in private and not scare the horses?

The lovers relish their rediscovery of erotic pleasure and sensual experience. They feel young again together. They just bought two pairs of pajamas, pink for her, blue for him.

Bless their good time and sharing, Jesus.

*Polite little notes on her birthday and at Christmas are killing Nan,
Jesus.* They come from her sister. These are the lasting evidence
of a twenty-year-old alienation.

Nan has long begged her sister to explain what initially
caused her to feel anger or betrayal. Year after year, birthday
following birthday, holiday after holiday, Nan feels helpless as
polite little notes pile up in the place of honest communication.

Nan wishes neither to dominate her sister nor intimidate
her, but hopes for an authentic relationship. Her hurt is deep.
Longevity increases stress and pain. It seems to Nan that her sister refuses to forgive something she apparently believes Nan
did to her in the past, yet she will not say what it was.

Nan does not know what it was.

Can all the polite little notes be replaced by honesty and
truth, Jesus?

At fifty-five, Dick still struggles from growing up in the be-seen-and-not-heard school of child rearing. But he's finally learned not to wait until people are at death's door to let them know how he feels, Jesus.

So he shares such expressions as "You look great in that color," "So kind of you to call," "I appreciated your letter," "You're special to me," and "I'm glad we're friends." Previously he'd only think of these things. Now he says them.

Dick experiences a great sense of liberation in expressing himself, Jesus.

Naomi has two children in their forties who show no regard for her.
They apparently don't want any kind of relationship.

Naomi believes she's a whipping boy for her son's failure in marriage. She does not want to hear someone say to her "Did you show them love?" In her opinion, she did. At eighty-two, she feels a strong need for her children to love her.

Yet when Naomi was in the hospital recently during an illness, her son—who lives two miles away—did not visit her or call. Her daughter doesn't want Naomi to spend any time with her two grandchildren.

Cruel silences seem to damage everybody involved here, Jesus. Can one of the people in this tragedy take the first step toward reconciliation and loving?

Joanna and Kathleen thankfully look back over thirty years of their loving relationship, Jesus.

As you know, their hardest obstacle at the start was not being seen as normative in the eyes of most other people. As lesbians, they were perceived as different, often as unacceptable.

What made it even more difficult then was that much of society dictated—or at least loudly whispered—that a woman was next to nothing without a man. This didn't give Joanna and Kathleen a very high place on the ladder of human and social acknowledgment.

However, they persevered, following in what they saw as your footsteps, Jesus, fashioning a life together woven in the example of your personal courage and unconditional love.

As always, Jesus, they ask for your blessing.

Bea spent nineteen years in an atmosphere of alcohol dependency and depression, Jesus. She's grateful for the change that has taken place.

For the past seven years she's been attending Al-Anon meetings. This has brought her very slowly but surely to loving herself and her husband.

In the past, Bea simply used to look for, and find, his bad qualities. Now she is learning to accept that no one, including herself, is perfect. In fact, she no longer allows his problem to remain at the center of her universe.

Although Bea does not like that he drinks almost daily, she is aware she's married to a practicing alcoholic who is a tender-hearted, sensitive human being with a fine sense of humor, a loving nature, and a deep love for her.

Bea continues to ask you for wisdom and guidance in her life, Jesus.

Albert, who is fifty-one, believes his parents relate to him as if he were a child of eight. It seems to him children were probably beyond his father's scope, and he shouldn't have reproduced. Albert is convinced both his sister and himself were burdens to both his parents.

So when Albert's mom and dad requested a visit this year, he turned them down. They were baffled and hurt. Albert tells friends he will breathe a huge sigh of relief when both his parents are gone, yet adds that he will never get over his guilt for feeling that way.

The hurts and problems revealed here seem bitter and ugly, don't they, Jesus? Can Albert walk a mile in his parents' shoes, and his mom and dad walk a mile in his? Can they communicate their feelings in a reasonable way and try to understand what is going on?

Connie says on her sixty-first birthday that she is making four life choices, Jesus.

The first is always to be learning something new. The second is to have enough going on in her life so that she doesn't spend a lot of time talking about the past. The third is to enjoy her own company. The fourth is to give back by doing some kind of volunteer work for others.

Please support her, Jesus, in her effort to view life as an opportunity, and then act on it.

Why do we let money be more important than it really is, Jesus? Can we keep it in perspective?

Daphne would like to do this, but anger dominates her life. Her daughter-in-law has not spoken to Daphne since marrying her son last year. Then, a few weeks ago, Daphne received the hard news that she is terminally ill.

Now she is confronted by decisions to make regarding her will. Daphne is rich, so she finds it hard to leave much of her wealth to her son, knowing he would share it with a woman who is alienated from her. Yet he's her only child, she loves him, and there is no one else close to her.

What seems important, Jesus, isn't either Daphne's will or the amount of money involved. Isn't it instead Daphne's human relationship with these two people, and theirs with her? Can Daphne, her son, and daughter-in-law, sit down and have the most serious talk of their lives? In the face of living and dying, can forgiveness be both offered and received, Jesus?

Now that he's retired, Jesus, Ralph finds the structure of his life has been blown to pieces. Work gave his life both meaning and identity. It also provided him with a second community away from home.

Ralph is afraid he's lost track of who he is, Jesus. Everything is blurred and moving too fast in his thoughts and feelings. Although Ralph has retired, he hasn't slowed down in his interior life. It seems to me that he needs to be reflective, search for fresh options, and even possibly try to do something he always wanted to do but had no time for.

Could you beckon him to turn a page in his life's story and begin a new chapter, Jesus? Is it possible Ralph might become someone different from who he thought he was?

WISDOM ॐ

I T REQUIRES MUCH WISDOM TO SURVIVE—AND LIVE. These prayers arise from men and women who face decisions. Some have already made constructive and positive ones. Others seem unable to accomplish this yet.

The latter remind me of someone standing on an ocean shore on a wintry day, having stripped to swim, yet powerless either to take the shock of the water or else climb into some warm clothes. Such a person, in utter frustration, blames the water, the air, the season, anything except oneself.

The point is: plunge or get dressed. In other words, make a decision. Wisdom helps us to do this.

As a couple, they seemed to have arrived at a dead end. Thelma retired from teaching to join her husband at home. Roy had retired two years earlier.

Roy's days were filled with going to the gym, reading, and watching TV. After she retired, Thelma could not relate to what he was doing. She grew unhappier daily, seemed at risk of losing her own sense of identity, and secretly pondered if they might have to separate and go their respective ways, Jesus.

A solution appeared when Thelma found a part-time job with flexible hours and people who became a community for her. It has let her feel she's an exciting part of life again instead of being out of the loop. An added incentive is her surprising rediscovery of an incentive to write.

All this has awakened a fresh sense of vitality in their life together as a couple. Roy and Thelma offer thanks, Jesus.

She used to think she needed a "someone" to fulfill her and make her happy. Now Eileen has come to the realization that she is a "someone" herself, Jesus.

When she gave up her trusted role of spectator, Eileen began to move in and do things when it was apparent they needed to be done. She became outgoing and friendly, in contrast to her former reclusiveness, believing that to have friends one must be an active friend.

Eileen's only regret is that she spent so much time in the past feeling sorry for herself. She's busily moving out of an isolated cul-de-sac in her life. She has been brought to her feet, energized by a new passion for life, in response to your grace, Jesus. Your gift is her changed life.

It's curious, Jesus. Some people feel lonely when they are alone. Others find the answer to loneliness in solitude. Still others feel lonely when they are with a companion or in a group of people.

Daniel was always shy and never really comfortable in social situations. Then his marriage broke up after thirty years. But finally he found a way of expressing himself, and breaking away from self-pity, in writing poems.

From out of the blue verse after verse came tumbling through his mind. Each contained reflections, thoughts, and feelings hidden deep inside him. This has seemingly enhanced a neglected quality of his life and given him purpose and direction.

Daniel is no longer alone, Jesus. He has found companions in his poems.

Estelle lives alone and likes it, Jesus. Into her seventies, she had a good marriage for a couple of dozen years to a man she describes as bright, humorous, and successful.

Widowed, she has held a dozen different jobs through the years, moved many times, and taken a score of night school classes. Estelle claims she loves to act and interact with anyone who will stand still long enough and not be intimidated by a seventy-plus sassy modern woman.

Living alone, Estelle explains, allows her to be sassy and do what she wants to do when she wants to do it—or not do it at all. She feels there is a lot to be said for not needing to do any compromising, explaining, accommodating, apologizing, or waiting on.

Bless Estelle in her sassiness, Jesus.

A gay man, Wayne is able to relax and accept himself for the first time in his life, Jesus. For many years he felt that he needed to play a role and give a long-run performance as a straight man.

Wayne tried hard to fit in nicely; listen quietly to offensive faggot jokes over lunch with business associates and not react; watch heterosexual couples hold hands in public, but never do the same thing with a gay partner; and never make anyone angry.

Now Wayne has found that he is able simply to be himself. He doesn't even have to be a witty and charming gay role model in yet another kind of performance. It's wonderful never having to lie about his identity in order to find peace.

Wayne is alive, and well, and living on his own terms. He offers thanks, Jesus.

Lucille is a widow, retired, and lives in her own home. However, she is not alone. Betsy, her forty-year-old daughter, lives with her.

This is not a promising situation, Jesus. Betsy sleeps until noon most days, does not work, is not looking for a job, and apparently has little or no interest in finding one. She doesn't dress and go out, but wears a robe most days as she watches soap operas on TV. She does no house chores, contributes no money, and just eats whatever meals Lucille prepares.

Lucille feels victimized and believes Betsy has used her cynically for years. Yet Lucille doesn't know how to correct the problem.

Is it possible for Betsy to become self-reliant, Jesus, and try to help her mother? Can Lucille quit playing a tired martyr role and speak the truth in love?

*Kevin lives in a huge condo complex that houses four hundred people,
Jesus.* Sometimes he tells friends "Talk about being in a lonely
crowd!" Many of the four hundred are alone. But instead of
reaching out to each other—connecting and helping—lots of
these women and men keep to themselves.

They seem to fear making a commitment to anyone or anything. The idea of intimacy apparently arouses fear in them, even
though they yearn for it.

Kevin has taken a close, long look at this situation. He realizes,
Jesus, that he can remain isolated, stubborn, self-centered, and
alone or else reach out to these other people and invite them into
his own life.

While he wants to reach out, Jesus, he acknowledges he
needs your help.

*She's grateful that she lives in a small town in the country where, in her
opinion, people are able to feel younger in old age.* But sometimes
Elsa must travel into the larger world. Here, she feels people
see her only as an older woman and stereotype her.

For example, the blue jeans and faded shirts Elsa wears at
home are often seen by strangers as sloppy and undignified.
Elsa says the looks she gets, Jesus, tell her she's seen as peculiar,
an older woman not conforming to a dress code or prescribed
pattern of behavior.

Yet isn't aging about wisdom and grace, Jesus, instead of
appearance?

Tony and Louise have been married forty-plus years and now exist in virtual silence, Jesus. Although they view each other's opinions and comments with contempt, they sleep together in the same double bed. They avoid touching and there is no communication. Half is his, half is hers.

Louise cooks the meals while Tony washes the dishes.

In earlier years, when Tony was often on the road with his sales job, Louise told him she was certain he had another woman in every city he visited. No matter how hard he tried to convince her that he never cheated, she remained sure he did.

Lack of trust did great damage, but Tony and Louise have shared good memories as well as bad ones. Will they be able to focus on a shared memory and history that bring them together? Can they realize life is slipping away from them quickly, and is precious?

As soon as Irene retired she felt reborn with a whole new life ahead of her, Jesus.

She has more interests and hobbies than she can handle. Right away she helped organize a food pantry, volunteered at a hospice, and regularly visits a nearby nursing home. Irene likes people and wants her life to have meaning in service to them.

The bottom dropped out of her life a few years ago when her husband of twenty-three years left her for a younger woman. Soon, however, Irene realized her biggest challenge was to avoid bitterness and find happiness. She concentrates on remembering things she is thankful for. She tries to be joyful instead of sad.

Please nurture her new hope, Jesus, and the renewed purpose in her life.

HEALTH: BODY, MIND, AND SOUL ॐ

T HESE ARE VERY SERIOUS PRAYERS. As we grow older, health issues become paramount in ways they usually never did before.

Such issues cannot be avoided. They will not go away. We must face them.

Our attitude, then, is of major importance. Confronted by pain, what can we do about it? Aware of a need to forgive some-one—as much for our own state of health as someone else's—how can we get started?

We find that body, mind, and soul are not separate entities. Our life is a network combining elements of these, and holding them together. A physical pain is linked to an emotional reac-tion as well as a mind-set and our spiritual well being.

The pain won't stop, Jesus. I've tossed and turned in bed all night, trying to get into a comfortable position. There doesn't seem to be one. I try to focus on something else, anything else, in an effort to shut this out of my mind.

The pain remains. I get up, move around, walk into the next room. Turn on a light, sit in a chair, and—in the middle of the night—try to read a book. Can I forget the pain? Apparently not.

Now I return to my bed. I breathe deeply—slowly, regularly in and out—and find such a focused exercise is helpful. I try not to think about the next hour, or day, but stay here fully with you, Jesus, in this moment.

Thank you for sharing my human nature. Your suffering and death on the cross gives me an undying example of your faith. Teach me, Jesus, to share your suffering and your resurrection.

My sense of humor is slowly returning, Jesus. Please work with me to keep myself in perspective, will you?

Lately it seems I've been taking a lot of things—including myself—far too seriously.

I made the terrible mistake of preparing a list of personal objectives that I virtually set in cement. Nothing, I told myself, could be permitted to stand in my way of achieving them—including other people's feelings or my own imperfect struggle for perfection.

This led to great problems. Some people got angry at me, while others left me strictly alone. Then someone kindly pointed out that I was acting ridiculous and was, in fact, very, very funny.

When the smoke cleared I saw the damage I was doing. I had placed my own ego, and its presumed needs, far ahead of your absolute priority to love my neighbor as myself.

You offer to heal my wounds and resolve my unresolved feelings. Give me the strength to reach out and take your outstretched hand, Jesus.

I seem to be in a mental or emotional labyrinth, concentrating on past failures and embarrassments, mistakes in judgment, and nightmares of every variety. I play old tapes in my head.

It seems clear I've been unduly self-centered, indifferent to the needs of others, and stubbornly unforgiving.

One negative memory after another is piled up. This makes me feel insecure and ashamed. I've been in a dark and dank place with shadows and goblins. Yet even as I fear it here, I know that you are with me.

You are the light. Please let me see the light.

I'm healing my body, mind, and soul by walking in the hills. I follow a dirt road that climbs randomly like a winding ribbon.

My body relaxes as my mind lets go of anxieties. I am at peace.

Exercise like this is essential for my well being, Jesus. I am grateful for it. I try to take good care of my body. A sigmoidoscopy revealed I need to take more fiber. I'm taking it. Allergy tests led to the need for regular treatment. I'm taking it. More tests showed my esophagus must be pampered. I'm pampering it. Glaucoma requires care. I'm caring for it. Osteoarthritis needs all kinds of treatment. I'm treating it.

I sit down on a large rock for a few moments. Concerns fall away. I am refreshed, energized, and gaze nonchalantly at playful clouds that enjoy resembling monsters in the sky.

Thanks for this freedom.

My soul tells me to slow down, say a prayer, and meditate, Jesus. This brings a real change in my life because I had been listening to another voice that demanded "Do it now!" Another voice exclaimed, "Beat the competition! Stay in the fast lane! Race to the finish line!"

My soul says not to.

My soul says the journey itself is what matters instead of the finish line.

My soul tells me to seek peace, not battle.

My soul says it is foolhardy to win the world if, as a result, I might lose my soul.

I am in an unhealthy state, Jesus, because I can't seem to forgive some-one. I admit the reason is that I am sitting in judgment on this person. I am angry.

I felt a betrayal of friendship. Yet, truly, I do not know all the circumstances. Admittedly, I jumped to conclusions, which don't seem either clear or obvious to me now. However, I don't know how to let down my guard. How can I confess this publicly? I might get clobbered. Isn't it safer to appear strong, even warlike?

I can't let anyone but you know, Jesus, how crazy this whole situation is. You see, a big part of my sitting in judgment on this person is that I can't stand his success. It cuts into my pride. I envy him.

Is there any way I can get out of this bad spider's web? I realize I weaved it myself. What a mess I've made of everything. I wish I could turn over this situation to you. Will you clean up my act, Jesus?

How can I explain to a casual acquaintance or a stranger that I am experiencing a bad day instead of a good one, Jesus?

Sleep deprivation seems to be at the bottom of all this. If I awaken in the middle of the night, and can't get back to sleep, the odds are that tomorrow will be a bad day. In the first place, I'll be fatigued. This will allow me a low tolerance for aches and pains, and coping with rough edges of life that can appear without warning.

Under such circumstances my sense of balance is impaired. So is my flexibility, optimism, and courage. Sometimes I think it would help a lot if I could hold up a sign reading "Please approach me cautiously today" or "Sorry, I'm not quite up to par today."

Because I have no such signs, it seems I must rely on the kindness and understanding of you and the people out there, Jesus.

Please tame my mind, Jesus, and connect it to reality. While letting it hold onto its dreams, keep it in line with my body and soul, Jesus.

My mind seems to be telling me to belie my years, turn back the clock, and abruptly occupy a body that hasn't resembled my own for more time than I care to remember.

You see, my mind is trying to sell me on the idea to begin a project that appeals to my ego, yet doesn't make sense in terms of the realities of my aging.

I enjoy being appreciated. There are moments when I quite sincerely wish I could turn back the clock thirty or forty years. A fantasy projection whispers to me not to acknowledge my age or condition.

Limitation is a word I've always tended to shun. It implies that I am not Alexander the Great, Julius Caesar, or Christopher Columbus. However, I know that I'm not, Jesus.

A serious moment can be helped by inherent humor, can't it, Jesus?

My knee hurts today. It's hard to walk up stairs, get up from a table or chair, and extremely awkward to climb in or out of a car.

Medical diagnoses of this condition have differed. Everyone agrees it's osteoarthritis, but there are varying views of the cause or treatment. Physical therapy provided some immediate relief, although it yielded no long-term results.

Walking itself is a chore this morning. Ironically it's painful to stand up, sit down, or lie down. I realize that fixating on the problem is a mistake because then it becomes obsessive.

I laughed out loud at my predicament when I attended a meeting today. Several of us sat on chairs in a circle. When the others stood up, I needed assistance. Then someone offered me a hand and literally pulled me to my feet. Both of us laughed.

It happened this morning as I stood in my garden. Death suddenly jumped out from behind a bush, just when the thought came to me that one day the roses will still be here—but I won't.

Such awareness is not new. However, in this particular moment, it became sharply real. Somewhat ingenuously, I asked: Is it fair for the roses to remain when I can't?

Other thoughts followed in similar fashion. Will I be able to accept death gracefully? With understanding? The years ahead of me are far fewer than those in the past. I pray for positive acceptance of my condition.

After I depart, the roses will manage very well without me, won't they, Jesus?

THANKSGIVINGS ॐ

E XPRESSING THANKS REQUIRES GRIT, EARNESTNESS, AND HARD WORK. A big reason is that it tests our fragile humility. Often we don't wish to acknowledge that we stand in need of someone else or others.

More than fifty years ago, I failed to say "thank you" to my high school English teacher. She spent hours patiently working with me. I wish I had been able to say "thank you" and to see her sensitive face light up in a moment of joyful response.

Neither is it easy to accept thanks. I often find it difficult because, like a lot of other people, I am acutely aware of my own shortcomings. I am embarrassed by being offered too much effusive thanks.

There is another dimension of thanks that it is easy to overlook. When we are engaged with God in prayer, many times we are asking for something instead of saying simply, "Thank you."

Here are thanksgivings.

I am thankful for memories, Jesus, realizing that I have responsibility and a role in creating them.

Special moments and events that occur in my life fill me with joy, challenge me, compel me to make decisions, and grow. If I don't acknowledge and appreciate such moments they may disappear rapidly and be forgotten.

It is my task to focus on them, take careful note of their complexity and patterns, and savor their presence in my life.

Your grace grants me the opportunity to transform such moments and events into memories. Hopefully they will stay with me always. I cherish this gift from you, Jesus.

When I was blessed with a free will in my creation, Jesus, I was entrusted with the treasure of forgiveness. It seems to me it amazingly resembles a muscle in my own body: I may choose to exercise it or not.

So I may offer forgiveness or refuse to do so. I may accept forgiveness or disdain it.

Whenever I freely offer forgiveness to someone, I am saved from bitterness, pride, and anger. However, when I do not offer forgiveness, I find myself withdrawing into an illusion of perfectionism. (I am perfect! I also expect it from others!)

Whenever I refuse to accept forgiveness from someone else, I commit myself to the tragedy of useless civil war without end.

Thank you, Jesus, for using forgiveness to remind me that I share humanness with other people, and also with you in your incarnation.

When I was young I came close to being killed in a car crash. It occurred during a violent snowstorm when visibility was reduced to near zero.

I was blinded by snow swirling in front of my eyes. Another car loomed up before me suddenly on a highway. After the crash, my car slid on ice out of control. It landed in a ditch, overturned, and spun.

Amid total silence my life seemed to stop. I reached tentatively for a leg, an arm, and slowly opened my eyes, wondering: Am I alive, am I here, am I whole?

When I realized that I had been spared, and was not hurt badly, I offered thanks for the gift of life.

I still offer it, Jesus. I am grateful for the opportunity to live long, grow into maturity, and acquire needed wisdom along the way. Thank you for enabling me to continue interacting with you and others. My journey, the adventure of a long life, fills my heart with gratitude.

I confess, Jesus, that I love some friends more than I like them. I like some friends more than I love them. Yet I am grateful for all of them.

I am continually astonished by their diversity. Some friendships are comforting and nurturing, while others challenge me and force me to struggle. Some friendships offer me security and meet my needs, while others require me to make sacrifices and receive little or nothing in return.

What all of them have in common, Jesus, is a sharing of life in the present moment. Mutuality is found here. I am grateful for these companions on my life's journey, Jesus. They safeguard me from rigid pride and crippling aloneness. Friendships are among my greatest blessings.

Thank you for the wonder of life, Jesus. I have found it in surprising and wonderful places: seasons, transformations, beauty, passion, energy, and creativity.

I've found it also in small things.

This reminds me of a time when I was a boy and had a dog named Laddie and a cat named Loretta. One of them was lovingly patient, surprisingly easily hurt, and endeavored to meet my every need. The other was mysterious, puzzling, secretive, often impatient, and wished me to meet its every need.

One obeyed orders, retreated when ordered, slept as late as I did, and generally left a good impression on guests. The other awakened me at dawn by climbing on my pillow and purring, often disobeyed or ignored orders, and seemed to enjoy scaring guests or making a poor impression.

One wagged a tail in devotion; the other rotated a tail in irritation. One licked my hand affectionately; the other sat on my lap and scratched my knee. One needed to be bathed by me; the other attended itself to such an intimate matter.

I remain thankful for their presence in my life, Jesus.

Several men and women have been great exemplars and role models for me, Jesus. Looking back, I realize how they made significant contributions to my life and development.

Mary E. Lowe taught me English. She was a plain woman who had never married, wore glasses, had no time for small talk, practiced discipline, and changed my life by virtually compelling me to write.

Dr. Walter King made house calls, healed minds and souls as well as bodies, worked with calm efficiency, and inspired confidence, including mine.

Amelia Scherrer was the epitome of grandmotherliness. Although our ages were vastly different, she accepted me unequivocally as an equal during my high school years. Probing with her disarming intelligence, she conveyed an image of an ordered, civilized way of life.

Paul Roberts, strong as a seasoned oak, was the finest pastor I ever knew. His smile was unforced, spontaneous, and contagious. He stood courageously for justice amid all sorts of human controversies. He represented the gospel message of light shining in darkness.

Elsie B. Essex was my history teacher. I was a shy kid who needed encouragement. She offered it during many an afternoon when she stayed late in her classroom to engage me in conversation, listen to what I had to say, and help me grow up.

I give thanks for these people in my life, Jesus.

I thank you for the center of peace that lies deep within me, Jesus. Here, conflicting voices and sounds of the world fade away. Here, complex puzzles and problems find resolution.

You heal me in this place, Jesus. Then you send me out into the mainstream of life again to continue serving you and helping others.

At times when I have been wounded by life and my energy was sorely depleted, you stayed with me here. You made no demands on me. You listened to me patiently. You bound up my wounds.

I have long felt your presence here. You held my body. You calmed the gyrations of my mind. You instructed me how to continue my journey with you.

Thank you for understanding, Jesus.

Faith has always been the anchor of my life, Jesus, even in difficult moments when I did not recognize it.

There was a time in school when I believed that I had turned completely away from you. The church seemed unrealistic and irrelevant. I balked at responding to your teachings. I didn't want any authority or discipline in my life. Freedom seemed to be exactly, and only, what I wanted to do.

Later, in young adulthood, a crisis developed when I still tried to force life to operate solely on my own terms. I experienced anguish and failure. What was I to do? Where could I go for an answer? Then I found you in my life again. You had never gone away.

Recently, when I was older and feeling battered by anxieties that grew out of my experience of aging, you reached out your hand firmly. You offered me once again the transformative gift of faith.

I find it the essential quality of my life, and thank you.

I used to say hope springs eternal, yet I have learned it doesn't, Jesus. Without you, hope can't reach far enough. It lacks sufficient energy. It has no depth.

Although morning automatically follows night, it cannot alter a condition of hopelessness simply by being there. Hope by itself cannot heal a desperately sick relationship, provide recovery for an addict, make peace in a warlike situation, or initiate dialogue between two people trapped by inchoate rage.

Only you can provide the spark that will enable hope to come alive in such a situation. You work with us when we are imprisoned in a morass of evil and despair, and teach us how to go on. You work patiently with us in our various addictions, one step at a time, restoring a vision of possibility and wholeness. You establish criteria for peace in our warlike scenes, teaching us discipline and compromise. After we vent our rage, you show us the absurdity and self-destruction we've been wallowing in. Then you enable us to communicate in open, honest ways.

Thank you for giving life to hope, Jesus.

Love originates with you, Jesus. I am incapable of loving without you. However, I don't really want to admit this. I wish that I could stand up as a paragon of nobility, achievement, and loving—all by myself—on my own two feet. As you know, I can't.

Left to my own desires, I must acknowledge that I have many failures. For example, whenever I envy someone in an irrational but consuming way, I allow envy to cloud my vision and become an enemy of love. I also am disturbed to realize when I exploit and manipulate someone else for my own advantage.

I come helplessly to you in this moment. I am fully aware that the good I would do, I am not doing. Just as troubling, the evil I don't wish to do, I am doing.

This dilemma is too much for me. Although my pride stubbornly maintains I am self-sufficient, I cry out for your help, Jesus. Thank you for answering my prayer by teaching me how to love.

CRIES
FROM THE
HEART ℘

SOME LIVES SEEM HARDER, MORE TESTED AND DIFFICULT, THAN OTHERS.

Men and women who are seemingly trapped in such situations appear to come close to hopelessness or despair.

Their prayers are, quite literally, cries from the heart. These are unvarnished prayers, specimens of raw life. I remember the prayer of a woman whose husband died in great pain after a long bout with cancer. She told me of her prayer. It was an outburst of pain, anger, loss, and helplessness. I realized that some people might be offended by its bluntness. At the same time, I honestly believed God received her prayer with compassion, deep understanding, and love.

As prayers, cries from the heart ask for guidance, strength to take a needed next step; a sliver of light in blackness, a sign of love in what appears a harsh or even loveless situation.

She is sick of widows crying about their loneliness. This, when they sit in warm houses with a fireplace, a dog, family album, and a big car in the driveway.

Marianne had to give away her dog because her apartment house does not permit pets. She found that family albums get scattered when one moves from a large house to a one-bedroom apartment. Marianne is broke and wonders how she can live and pay for medical insurance. She is bitter because she lacks a house, a car not falling apart, money to fix a car, or just one normal holiday.

Be with Marianne in her anger, Jesus. Please help her to cease comparing her life with that of others, especially when she has no idea what their real lives are like.

Stewart has fought the battle of low self-esteem for as long as he can remember. He could never seem to measure up to his father's demands of achievement or his mother's unrealistically lofty expectations.

Worse, his siblings were stars while he wasn't. His brother was popular, an athlete, and president of his class in school. His sister was a beauty queen and smart enough to be awarded a college scholarship. Stewart did the best he could but never earned recognition, honors, or stood out in a crowd.

Now in his sixties, Stewart seems unaware that the greatest obstacle to fulfillment or peace is his search for perfection in life. Yet he demands it of others, especially his children and associates at work. Saddest of all, Jesus, he demands it of himself, and invariably considers himself inferior, inadequate, a failure in life.

Please help Stewart to accept himself as he is—a man whom you accept and love, Jesus.

Agnes has lived nearly a half-century in a lonely marriage. In 1940 her husband boasted that for a two-dollar marriage license, he got sex on demand, a clean house full of kids, and his clothes always mended. Plus she took care of the chickens and the garden.

Their marriage vows stressed the word "obey." She began to wither. Through the years their home filled with children, all taught to love and respect and obey their father. Agnes was lonely.

She still is, Jesus.

Can her husband grow up, look around, see a new reality, begin to understand the concept of mutuality and sharing, find a way to express love that Agnes can comprehend?

Because Agnes feels unfulfilled and joyless, can she come to a sense of her own humanity and human rights, and take a step toward freedom?

Can you wake them up, Jesus?

Ben has arranged to have a drug available that he can self-administer and take his life when, or if, he chooses. He says he fears only one thing: being a burden to others by virtue of a stroke or Alzheimer's.

He believes it is hypocritical of anyone to deny him that choice, Jesus. Ben is someone with a lot of strength but also a reflective side. He has written instructions for his funeral, requesting Mozart piano concertos and, thinking of his family's financial resources, a cheap coffin.

Ben wants a burial space so people can come to visit. He worries about not having everything in order when he dies, leaving behind what he calls a mess for others to have to clean up.

Please help Ben to prioritize life over death, Jesus, and to celebrate fully the present moment while he has it.

Childhood for her was a "Mommy Dearest" kind of situation, Jesus. In the middle of the night her mother would appear with a wooden coat hanger or heavy wooden hairbrush, and beat her and her sister. Her mother seemed to enjoy it and laughed at their terror.

When the two girls, brutalized and anxious, tried to tell others about what their mom did, they were admonished: What bad things had they done to upset their mother? Scared of her and numbed by his life experiences, their father never said a word in the girls' behalf or confronted his wife.

Once, after a beating, their mother said: "What kind of monster do you think I am that I would do this to you if you didn't deserve it?"

A great deal of childhood pain needs a lot of healing, doesn't it, Jesus?

The absence of a loved one is a cruel loss, Jesus. Marie has five children and four grandchildren with whom she spends much of her time. She also has a part-time job, lots of friends, and hobbies.

But by Sunday evening after a quiet weekend that includes attending church, she finds herself in tears. She misses her husband, who died last year. Her life has become a strange and unfamiliar place.

Help her, Jesus, to mourn her loss and express her grief, understanding that she's like the rest of us—all of us who need to grieve, when we must, in our own time.

Help others to treat Marie with sensitivity and love while she is mourning and hurting.

Then, when the time is right, please reveal to Marie how she may find herself in a new life drama with a revised script, Jesus.

On the verge of his second divorce, Edgar feels brokenhearted, disappointed, and lonely. However, the reason is not his divorce. It's his children.

There are four. All have families and careers. Edgar is convinced they don't care a whit about him. For the past fifteen years he believes they knew he was having a very, very difficult time, yet none ever expressed any concern or offered to help.

Edgar is bitter because, as he sees it, their childhood was filled with happiness, love in abundance, a full-time mother, and a father who provided them an upper-middle-class lifestyle. He wonders why his kids refuse now to communicate with him when he needs them.

Has the moment come for Edgar to seek out his children and listen to what they have to say? Try to grasp their actual feelings, hear their real stories? Perhaps he can learn something new, Jesus. Maybe all of them can make needed changes in their lives.

Gertrude is in a rut, Jesus. She describes herself as one of those unfulfilled, languishing souls who feels life has passed her by.

Nothing seems to work for her. She feels she is a reject, left out of the mainstream, a case of life run aground.

Yet does she let others know what her feelings are? While she stays secretly frustrated and unfulfilled, often they mistakenly are led to think she is fine.

Maybe, if she can open up to a few friends whom she trusts, Gertrude can arrive at a better approach to living. Can she start moving toward that goal slowly, patiently, steadily?

Before his elderly mother died, Herbert gave up literally everything to care for her. As soon as he got home from work he was by her side, trying to meet her every need, listening to what she had to say.

However, he grew angry when she appeared not to be grateful. Always she seemed to want more, more, more. Herbert let his mother know that he was frustrated and felt she was ungrateful. Then she died. Now he cannot forgive himself.

Herbert does not seem to understand that forgiveness is essential, Jesus, and self-forgiveness is a large part of it. None of us can allow our yesterdays to dominate our todays and tomorrows, can we, Jesus?

Philip and Christina's son wrote to them last year saying he never wished to see or hear from them again.

They have not heard from him since. He changed his phone number after they tried to call. From their standpoint, all this happened without warning and for no apparent reason. A part of their heartbreak is that they are not permitted any interaction with their grandchildren.

In virtually any situation, Jesus, aren't there different points of view to take under consideration? It seems to me that nowhere is a spirit of generosity and openness more needed than in conflicts between older parents and their adult offspring.

Will you help them to listen to one another, Jesus, and to try to figure out why they feel the way they do?

Mel never used to be afraid, Jesus. Always he was hearty, robust, a natural leader, and someone to whom others turned for support. It would never have occurred to Mel to fear virtually anything.

However, his life began to change with passing years. His wife became an invalid with a long illness before she died. Their children grew up and moved away, and a beloved daughter dropped out of his life when she was killed in an automobile accident.

Mel was forced to leave a job he liked because he'd reached a stipulated retirement age. Then, he left his old home for a small apartment. He still has a number of acquaintances and a few friends, but feels his life has shrunk. Now he discovers certain fears that he feels did not exist before. Fear of isolation. Fear of growing older. Fear of dying alone.

Mel has started to let a light burn all night in a room next to where he sleeps. He leaves the door ajar because the light comforts and assures him when his sense of aloneness becomes overwhelming. Will you let Mel know you are with him, Jesus?

HARD
QUESTIONS ❧

T HESE PRAYERS ARE REALLY QUITE ORDINARY. They occur
from time to time in everybody's life.

Confronted by the vicissitudes of life, all of us ask hard
questions. A seemingly impassable gulf looms ahead—and our
prayer sounds like "What can I do?" Or, we've dropped into a
dark emotional pit that offers no obvious exit, and we ask "How
in the world can I get out of this place?"

Hard questions occur regularly in a world of complex
human relationships, kids, jobs, traffic, money problems, ambi-
tions, failures, and the often threatening humdrum of daily life.

Caught between a rock and a hard place, we pray.

*Although her children have been grown and gone from home for years,
Martha still feels responsible for things that happen to them.*

She explains that she believes firmly in letting go. However,
she finds it extremely hard when a daughter's sad appearance
expresses great anxiety and pain. Her daughter's seeming mistakes haunt and trouble Martha.

However, her daughter's ambivalence about her mother's
involvement in her life brings Martha conflicting messages.
One time her daughter seems to want motherly advice. The
next time, her daughter informs Martha to quit meddling.

Can they find a common ground for communicating, Jesus?
Caring and concern seem natural and good. Yet when they
become instruments of manipulation and control, they can be
troubling. Martha and her daughter seek help to find a proper
balance, Jesus.

Aging has hit Victor in the face with a number of recent deaths, Jesus. First, there was his father-in-law, a hale and hearty seventy-nine. Then his older and only brother at sixty-two. And one of his closest friends at eighty.

Now he watches the rapid disintegration of his mother's intellect from Alzheimer's disease, and her panic and determination as she tries to hold on.

Victor does not fear death, Jesus, but helplessness and pain, loss of dignity and limbo. Sometimes he thinks about the possibility of having dementia and lying in his own feces in a nursing home. He describes the terror he feels then as being akin to seeing Godzilla peering in his window.

Comfort Victor in his fear. Make him know that he is held firmly in your everlasting arms of eternal strength. Help him to focus on your unconditional love, Jesus.

Although she's only thirty-six, Betty tells friends that she feels old sometimes. She sees physical changes in herself that she never thought could happen. These have been difficult to accept.

Sometimes Betty buys into the age discrimination that says a woman can't be beautiful past a certain age. More than that, she wonders if she has sufficient faith, fortitude, and courage to grow even older than she already is.

She's a single mom, divorced with a young daughter. Her job requires a lot of her. She worries about the future.

With any luck, Betty is going to wake up to a number of future birthdays. Forty-six. Fifty-six. Sixty-six. Seventy-six. My point is, Jesus, that she's going to need to understand that different people have to approach aging in individual ways.

Please help Betty to stop looking at people in terms of what their age is. There are so many other things to look for, aren't there, Jesus?

Joe doesn't like to feel he's being herded in a group of older men and women. It isn't that he does not enjoy them. But he dislikes occupying what he calls a ghetto populated exclusively by people who are his own age.

The truth is that Joe has a certain fear of aging, Jesus. It cuts against his desired image. He tells friends he's going to die on the day after he gets old. That day will come, he explains, when he no longer admires a shapely leg, curvaceous hips, a well-turned breast, and his blood is no longer stirred by an enticing smile.

Help Joe to understand, Jesus, that virility and acting like an eternal playboy are by no means the sole indicators of the fountain of youth.

How can we learn to say what we mean, Jesus? Sometimes when we say "I feel fine," we're telling a lie. Or we may say "There's really no need to talk about that," yet know there is a great need. We may blurt out "Do what you want, I don't care," while we really care very, very much.

Do we fail to communicate because we're frustrated and tired? Are we trying to simplify a complicated situation? Yet we may only create more confusion and hurt, and undermine credibility.

Help us, Jesus, to hear what another person really means in place of mere words. Help us to say what we mean. Enable us to understand body language, our own and that of others: a fist clenched, a foot firmly positioned on the floor, eyes hard. Can we comprehend someone's show of anger may be a hidden plea for patience and love, support and understanding? Help us to get the message, Jesus.

Jean thought she and her daughter were the best of friends, Jesus. This changed when Jean stayed with her daughter for two weeks after her baby was born.

Jean was shocked and hurt when her daughter seemed to treat her as an intruder. While putting away some maternity clothes Jean inadvertently opened an unsealed box. Later her daughter stared at her coldly and said "Before you open any boxes, will you ask me?" Jean felt her daughter had changed completely and become a different person.

But, Jesus, is it possible her daughter only felt a compelling need to occupy her own space and give it certain boundaries? And, is it also possible the incident brought up her daughter's memories of ways Jean may have acted in the past as her mother? Was her daughter trying to tell Jean that she'd looked forward for many years to having her own home, or perhaps that she was just worn out physically from the delivery?

It seems to me that love extends far beyond territorial rights, and sometimes may even cancel them, Jesus. Do you think so?

Ernest dreamt about retirement for many years. It seemed that, at the end of the rainbow, he could finally relax, enjoy security, do what he wished, spend golden years with family and friends, and become a wise and happy old man.

However, Ernest received a hard wakeup call, Jesus, when it became apparent he couldn't afford to do any of these things. Instead he must continue working in order to make a living and pay bills.

He is puzzled, annoyed, and frustrated that he has to keep up with what he calls the rat race, Jesus.

Can you help him come down a few decibels so that he can stop panicking, center himself, and try to find some options? Maybe there's another occupation in which he can find considerably greater satisfaction. Possibly he can learn some new skills.

Ernest seems to be looking at a solid brick wall, with no apparent outlet, and he feels despair. Will you tell him about the possibility of reinventing himself? The challenge could bring him joy and fulfillment. Will you awaken him to new life, Jesus?

Marc's mom, eighty and in excellent health, is right in the middle of her children's lives, and it's driving them crazy, Jesus. According to Marc, she has no stop button.

She calls Marc several times a day. With his own life and needs, he feels pushed beyond endurance. Because he loves his mother, he finds the situation heartbreaking.

In his view, his mother is a wounded woman who, when she was forty, neglected to make real friends and develop interests and hobbies. So, as she grows older, her life is empty.

Marc objects to the portrayal of adult children like himself as selfish and inconsiderate. On that basis, aging parents are seen as people who have been victimized or shelved. He says he wants to make his mother his friend, as his daughters have made him their friend.

Many people seem locked in long-playing human roles, Jesus. Can they step outside them and see themselves—and each other—in liberating and fresh ways?

Gene's retirement brought on a real crisis, defining life in vastly differ-ent ways for Thelma and himself.

In the first place, their life together slowed down consid-erably. At first they withdrew from a number of activities and cultivated quietness. They stayed close to home and members of their family.

Now they have begun to reach out and find new things to do. Thelma and Gene just attended his fiftieth class reunion. He tells friends how this smacked him in the face when he realized how much time these years represent in his whole life.

Thelma and Gene made the trip in their trailer. Thelma says they're both far more spoiled then they are aware by having all the comforts and conveniences of home in what they call their fifth wheel.

Bless their last years, Jesus.

Maude finds herself in the midst of a communication crisis with her mother. She sees her mother as a sad, neurotic woman who considers herself a total failure in life, yet (at the same time) is extremely self-centered.

While Maude continues to visit her mother out of a sense of duty and moral conviction, she believes there is no possibility of real communication. She has been unable to find any words that make her mother feel valued and cared for.

Her mother, on the other hand, is mystified by what she perceives to be her daughter's arrogance, coldness, and highly judgmental attitude. She wonders: Why can't her daughter stop looking futilely for perfection in her—and just love her as she is? She asks: Why can't my daughter get over her rigid sense of duty and moral conviction, loosen up, be warm and intimate, and show a glimmer of love?

Can you help them to focus differently when they look at each other, Jesus?

Is it possible to forgive? Sheila asked the question after her divorce. She felt hurt and bitter. Had she thrown away the best years of her life for nothing? Now she found herself alone when she'd assumed she would enjoy companionship, security, and a loving relationship.

Time passed. Sheila's feelings slowly mellowed. She remembered the good times as well as the bad ones.

Then she learned her former mate was seriously ill, required difficult surgery, and would be confined to his home during recuperation. He had no one to care for him.

When Sheila contemplated forgiveness, it occurred to her the commandment to forgive mentions no exceptions, Jesus. She gave up part of her vacation time to watch over him, deciding that she wished to invest time and energy in being friends.

It seems Sheila found an answer to a hard question, Jesus.

Don is dying. Everybody else has known it for some time. Now he knows it too.

He has had a stubborn, simple faith all his life. Don got it from his parents and early religious training, although he was never the regular churchgoer he sometimes wished to become.

Now he prays that his life may continue eternally after his body's death, Jesus. He longs to be reunited after death with loved ones and old friends. Don regrets his life's imperfections and wants to greet certain friends, long departed, whom he feels he hurt. His most longed-for gift is a deeper understanding of where he has already been and where he is going.

Don yearns to see you and be welcomed home, Jesus.

COURAGE ॐ

C OURAGE ALWAYS SEEMS RARE, yet probably occurs in countless situations we never hear about.

An outstanding witness to courage was provided by Dietrich Bonhoeffer, whom I admire as much as anyone else in the twentieth century. A German pastor and scholar, he was in the United States when Hitler rose to power in Nazi Germany. Bonhoeffer could have remained safely here. However, he returned to Germany, became an activist in the movement to destroy Hitler's power, and was hanged. His letters from prison are Christian classics, his ideas about religion major ones. He is a role model of courage.

Courage is found whenever anyone transcends limitations to meet a need or strive for a better state, against all odds. These prayers, in a sense, are profiles of courage.

The courage of sacrifice, of involvement, of simply being a responsible human being in a difficult moment, is a wonder of life.

Gloria is struggling to deal with immobilizing arthritis, Jesus. She's tried different medications, experienced up and down days, and sought a new center of interest in her life.

Her prayers were answered when she discovered a training program that enables her to work with a computer. Now she leaves her home with a walker at six-thirty most mornings. Then she catches a bus that carries her to a nearby class on time at a community college.

At first, she was afraid of the new routine and felt insecure about her health. But she persevered. She is aware how blessed she's been by entering into this whole new phase of her life.

Gloria hangs out happily with her younger classmates. Friendly and supportive, they represent an entirely new form of community in her experience. She used to find herself in an emotional dead-end situation where she was lonely and insecure.

Courageously, she continues to enable her fulfillment and joy, Jesus.

The ground beneath Zachary's sense of well being and security seemed to give way, Jesus. Big changes confronted him abruptly. He was terrified. Even worse, he didn't know what to do about it.

He prayed for a way to look ahead with hope and achieve some visible progress in making sense of his life.

All of a sudden he got the message, Jesus: Zachary could change the way he looked at life! He could open himself to fresh possibilities, discover new horizons, nurture clear thinking, and welcome different solutions.

Soon a positive attitude instead of one that spelled unhappiness and failure started making a difference in his life. Instead of grimly fighting life, Zachary began to embrace it.

Now Zachary finds he's able, day by day, to start from scratch in numerous ways. He thanks you, Jesus, for guiding him from his former terror to a new beginning.

Lillian refuses to be a has-been, Jesus. Her aging persona told some people that she was no longer someone with fresh ideas to be considered. They decided she deserved a back seat on life's bus.

She didn't accept their rejection.

"I know better," she said. She's crammed with knowledge that only years could bestow upon her. Lillian affirms that she's a person to be reckoned with.

"I count!" she exclaims. "Let me shout it from the steeples."

Be with Lillian in her robust liberation, Jesus. Enable her to share her freedom with others who need her message.

Looming retirement puzzles and threatens Bernard. It will take place in three years. Looking ahead, he is unable to see signs of the organized, meaningful life he presently finds as a full-time employee in a job he loves.

Bernard is aware that he needs—and wants—continuing zest and vitality as a hallmark of his life.

As a result, he plans to join the Peace Corps. He wishes, as always, to make a difference in the world. Also he needs an adventure. In fact, travel is his passion.

Bernard prays that after a tough, exhilarating experience abroad, he can sail into retirement with a flourish. His hope, Jesus, is to become better prepared to make his retirement a meaningful, joyful experience.

Devastated by several recent deaths, Melissa turned to a new focus of joy in her own backyard. She has discovered the wonder of becoming a bird watcher and feeding birds.

This led to yet another adventure when a squirrel came down from a tree to take some bread that she had left for the birds. However, on the very next day, Melissa forgot to put bread out. Looking through her kitchen window, she saw the squirrel seated on a fence rail, gazing her way. She thought it appeared a bit morose as well as hungry.

Melissa quietly walked outside and placed some bread on the grass. She observed the squirrel waiting for her to reenter the house. In the next moment it scurried down for its gift.

Melissa is grateful for finding comfort and emotional release in the simple drama unfolding in her own backyard, Jesus.

A widower in his sixties, Hank was feeling sorry for himself when he decided to attend a class reunion. To his surprise, he found Jean there.

They had dated for a while many years ago when they were both students at East High. Then he went away to college. They never saw each other again.

It was fun to renew their old friendship. He asked her for a date. They enjoyed each other's company. Finally, after several months, they explained to their somewhat startled but happy families they were in love.

Marriage followed. Hank is grateful for this second chance in life. He's learned there are more options open to him than he realized, Jesus.

"I love aging,"Claire says at sixty-four.

"It seems I have always been prepared to age. So it is hard for me to see myself as fitting the image of 'old' held by so many others. This is the best time of my life. I can be open, honest, selfish, or whatever I want. I keep my mind active. My spirit is positive. I plan to be one hundred."

Claire continues a long routine of volunteering her time, working to assist other people in need, and staying deeply involved in life.

Right now Claire is walking up the street, Jesus. There is a spring to her gait. She's smiling, looking around her, clearly someone who loves being vital and alive.

Greg always yearned for what he called the simple life, Jesus. He wanted quiet, closeness to nature, a slow pace, and time to go his own way and reflect on the beauty and meaning of life.

Yet his job for many years in the postal service in a large urban area plunged Greg into stress, a fast pace, and mounting duties. Finally, when he retired, he got up the courage to do what he had long wished.

After selling his condo, Greg used the proceeds to buy a new pickup and fifth-wheel trailer. Now he lives on a campground and has a storage shed on his lot for his belongings. Greg has no debts to worry about.

He has always loved the desert, Jesus. Here he sees blue skies every day. There is little traffic and no smog. Greg says he is sorry when he hears of unfortunate people who are not as happy as he is.

Bless Greg in his individuality, solitude, and the way of life he has chosen, Jesus.

Constance found a terrible void in her life after her husband died. She volunteered at a hospital, bowled twice a week, stayed active in church, and kept her home. But still, her life felt lonely, Jesus.

Then her twenty-three-year-old granddaughter showed vivacity, love, and courage with an invitation to Constance to keep Wednesday evenings open.

Over the past year they've taken turns cooking or else gone out to dinner. They have laughed and cried together, talking over their week's activities and how they assess what lies ahead in their lives.

The opportunity to grow closer is a great blessing, Jesus.

Paralyzed by multiple sclerosis and living in a convalescent hospital, Ursula has become a counselor to the staff in an unexpected way, Jesus.

Her mind is sharp, and she remains cheerful. The staff all love her. They have learned they can tell her about their personal problems and dilemmas while they care for her. Ursula listens intently and deeply. They know their stories will not be repeated. Totally helpless, she has become a remarkable listener. She has found her vocation. Her gift is a marvel.

Despite her physical helplessness, Ursula is able to do something for others, Jesus.

SPIRITUALITY
AND FAITH ॐ

A FTER WRESTLING ALL NIGHT WITH AN ANGEL—OR
GOD—in the book of Genesis, Jacob declared, "I will not
let you go, unless you bless me."

In our own day-to-day relations and encounters with God,
we find the deepest expressions of our faith. Also, in times of
crisis and passion in our faith journeys, we stand vulnerable and
naked before God.

There are even moments—rare and memorable—when,
like Jacob, we wrestle with God. These prayers grow out of that
kind of intimacy, the recognition of the presence of holiness in
our lives.

Mistakenly, I thought
my age and experience
shielded me from
shock and pain, Jesus

Yesterday,
someone I trusted
betrayed and hurt me
cruelly and imperiously

I reacted
retreating far inside myself
trying to block feeling

Yet I desired revenge

Could I face the world again
look into its mocking eyes?
I was embarrassed
and humiliated

Your eyes, Jesus,
did not mock me

Thank you for being with me
in your love

The running of the new day
has begun
Here is my hand

Old problems not resolved
come back to haunt us, don't they, Jesus?

I remember when I didn't tell the truth
my life was a significant one
it provided everyone an easy way out
conflict was averted but truth was buried

Must I remain
a contented phony, Jesus?
Can I allow your truth
to help me tell the truth?

What is truth, Jesus?
It's staggering, isn't it?
I'm tempted to define it
according to what I want

Help me not to do that, Jesus

I am grateful
for lessons learned
wisdom granted
a sense of serenity, Jesus

Demons used to plague my life
I was afraid of them
You taught me to name them
call each by its own name

Anxiety gave me no peace

Loneliness tortured me
I did not yet know the grace
of solitude
that transforms it

Insecurity made me restless

Pride laid siege to my life
making me see friends as enemies
fresh encounters as threats
servanthood as weak

You freed me from these powers

Thank you
for the renewal
of my life, Jesus

It would be so easy for me
simply to give up
a blanket of indifference beckons me
to lie down on it
and go to sleep

Why bother, Jesus?
why fight?
why struggle?

Yet I know
if I am not committed
to hope inside my own life,
I cannot contribute
to hope in the world

And, I realize
if I am not committed
to hope in the world,
I cannot contribute
to hope in my own life

Wrestle with me,
I pray you, Jesus
give me strength I need
bless me with courage

You call us to stand for
justice and peace, Jesus
in our later years
just as when we were young

Yet often we don't hear you
are selfish and preoccupied
turn our backs on the needs of others
do not wish to rock the boat

We have eyes to see, but do not see
ears to hear, but do not hear
mouths to speak, yet do not speak

We are afraid, Jesus
often we wish you would go away
leave us alone
so we'll not
have to become involved

Strengthen our bodies
to be instruments of
your mercy and justice

Strengthen our minds and wills
to be instruments of
your mercy and justice

Thank you, Jesus,
for revealing
the pattern of
your love and will

Some give up their search
grow tired and discouraged
fear a sophisticated puzzle
eludes their ability to solve it

Yet the pattern is simple, isn't it?

Blessed are the poor in spirit
those who mourn
the meek
those who hunger for righteousness

Blessed are the merciful
peacemakers
who are persecuted
the pure in heart

Yours is the power
and glory
now and forever

I cry out for wholeness as I grow older

I accept myself as one small part of your creation,
your plan of life, Jesus

Now I see through a glass, darkly

My peace requires union in you

I yearn for this with all my body, all my mind,
all my soul

I cry out, in my passion and need,
for the wholeness of communion with you

I hunger

I thirst

Thank you for loving
nourishing
sustaining me

Make us aware of new ways instead of old paths
This is our prayer

Jesus,
Lift us out of old hatreds and despairs
This is our prayer

Jesus,
Help us to offer honest and deep thanks
for life with you and other people
This is our prayer

Jesus,
Teach us how to make our prayers and lives
become one
This is our prayer

Jesus,
When our world chooses death over life,
show us how to choose life over death
This is our prayer

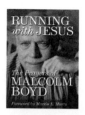

Running with Jesus by Malcolm Boyd
128 pages, 0-8066-4068-5

Readers will find in this book some of Malcolm Boyd's finest work. His honest approach to prayer has been inspiring the prayers of others for decades.

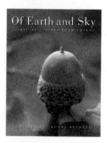

Of Earth and Sky: Spiritual Lessons from Nature
compiled by Thomas Becknell
160 pages, 0-8066-4260-2

A wonderful compilation of classic and contemporary selections from more than eighty of the world's finest writers to illustrate the seven virtues as they are taught in nature.

The Art of Growing Old by Carroll Saussy
176 pages, 0-8066-3617-3

This book is for adults interested in increasing life satisfaction. It emphasizes the importance of making plans and enacting those plans as the practical means to moving into the last decades of life with a sense of expectation and fulfillment.

Psalms for Healing by Gretchen Person
170 pages, 0-8066-4161-4

A thoughtful collection of the most helpful passages from the psalms for those who seek healing. These selections and prayers help people connect with the healing power of God.

Available wherever books are sold.
To order these books directly, contact:
1-800-328-4648 • www.augsburgfortress.org
Augsburg Fortress, Publishers
P.O. Box 1209, Minneapolis, MN 55440-1209